Tim Page

Mid-term Report

Thames and Hudson

FOR OUR NEWBORN JOY IN LIFE, A SON

KIT CLIFFORD PAGE,

BORN 19TH DECEMBER 1993

On the half title: Patpong, Bangkok, 1991
On the title page: High-school girls, Cuba 1988

British Library Cataloguing-in-Publication-Data
A catalogue record for this book is available from the British Library

ISBN 0-500-277958

Printed and bound in Singapore by CS Graphics

Mid-term Report

CONTENTS

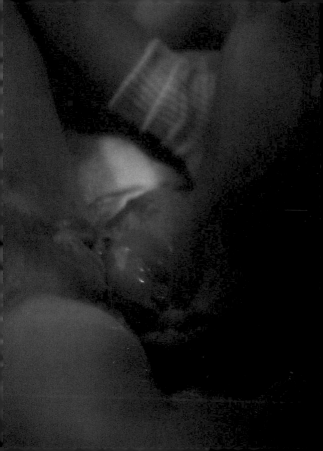

BIRTH AND CONFESSION

The images kaleidoscope together with an urgency born from nostalgia

the emotion of the taking blurring with the artistry only perceived after the event. The road, the adventure, the edge swirling into focus remain more sharply in the mind than the actuality laid out on the light table. The difficulty is to distinguish the moment from the frame. The photograph can virtually replace the reality. Looking now, fluorescent, cold, across these transparencies, will anything ever compare? Will a tranquillity, a harmony be achieved in a way that makes some particular images special? How often does some absolute, balanced, clear, poised knowledge say that now – as I squeeze this trigger/shutter – is the stroke that of a master, that a classic image of enduring properties will emerge from the chemical soup, pass its editorial tests and then enter the pages of history? Who is to discover and exploit it after it was an observed moment, consciously captured, the eye turned classically towards time?

The more I look across the light-table, the more radical does the selection become – so much thoughtless junk, frames snapped at whims forgotten, moments somehow dubbed just right, though, technically, poorly put together. Endless celluloid to be trashed, desecrated forever, carrying with it a remorseless sense of history as each is chucked into the waste bin below the editing surface. Oh that I could be so discriminating in all aspects of my life, so decided, so absolute in choice. Pleasant to imagine yourself so sussed to a sense of perfection, with such a weather eye to the eternal image that you are aware that you have crossed the bridge from information to art.

Am I to decide what has or has not crossed that bridge?… Who is to tell? Is it for our peers, or is there a photographic/art instinct? Like music and painting it has no constraints on its limits. A photographic image of quality impinges upon you, fixes you in time as can a melody, and can cause an emotive flash-back in the same way. A silly millimetre of shift in frame or focus is as discordant as a wrong note. Harmony of the right optical components, perspectives and considerations has to be observed as astutely as the musical scales; attuned to the timbre of life, the pulse of our inner selves, our souls.

Harmony, like wisdom, is apparently gained with experience and maturity, the essence of knowledge through age. That knowledge finds meaning in the ordinary and the norm, pleasure in simplicity, form and line in the oblique. Through such maturity comes knowing contentment in the creative moment. It means recognizing the sacred enlightened moment as is approaches.

During the war we were too busy surviving or over-mythologizing our immediate past after action captions or reports, too involved in the now to cogitate upon the future in a classic frameable sense. Editors demanded action and occasionally printed art. The still moments of the conflict were not as vendable, the contemplative harder to get to grace a LIFE double-spread. The horror of it, was always viable. (The glamour of it was played down, now unfashionable.) It was a transitional time, when monochrome coverage dissolved to colour, and was soon dominated by the television camera. The demonic box has come to circumscribe our impressions, as the picture-magazine did that of our elders. These moments, once forever captured, are now freeze-framed and pixeled to paper, discarded as mainly a forgettable continuum, a backdrop pablum to consumerism. For me, our human frailty is rarely portrayed with moving imagery – it remains the domain of the still photograph. Of that I knew very little until I plunged into the deep end of the pool of life, carrying the very *raison d'être*, a camera. The pool was Indo-China in the early '60s, sliding deeper into the Vietnam of 1965.

Vietnam will haunt forever. The same applies to the camaraderie of the war's survivors, a kinship that all who have endured trauma together have as a bond. Back in the US, that Vietnam bonding has

Chithurst, 1990

Kelaniya, Sri Lanka,
1983

Phnom Pen, 1990

now attained an almost radical chic mythical status after being denigrated for being even loosely associated.

Facing coming home, once daunting, was now merely a gateway to a separate happiness. As cathartic and stilling as passing into the subdued interior of a wat to sit quietly in front of the Buddha while other faithful glided past and around; in Vietnamese it spelt Hoa Binh – here we simply say 'Peace'.

Going to its consecration on Veterans Day '85 only stimulated being drawn back on every possible occasion. So far, four times. There is a comfort in being able to look at the pit of sadness and remember friends and comrades who perished, to re-tune to their spiritual and artistic energies and be able to rejoice in the 'now' of being alive.

With little or no knowledge of imagery, I found myself being presented for accreditation as a staff photographer for UPI in Saigon at the Rex hotel, which then housed JUSPAO (Joint United States Public Affairs Office) just after Tet of '65. An overland pre-hippy

post-beat trail tracing a Hesse-like path that had taken me to the East, an awakening never afforded by purely occidental learnings. The paradox of the Orient: on the one hand the philosophy that seeps into you unawares, on the other a foreign reality. The weirdest and most wondrous college of life a student could want for. I was plunged and steeped in a timeless sump, awoken to all that had only been vaguely conceived from reading romanticized accounts. Everything the opposite of the norm back in the early Sixties West, where just being had been a job, a work of survival, a craft adapted to wait any moment that would at any time present the obtuse. The best *aide-mémoire* was a classic grammar school education in an age when education still bore the precepts of being able to teach oneself, scan everything and assimilate what you personally needed, of how to glean knowledge from the countless passing collages.

My upbringing was free of encumbrances, with affiliations only as tenuous as I wanted them to remain. A rearing of benevolence y already outmoded, although still adhered to. An independence adhered to. An independence guaranteed, the freedom to explore granted, a curiosity, and intrigue surrogated implanted. Selfishly accepted, I had taken all the profferings. Forged upon them to rue greed of consumption, karmically destitute and adrift. Unfocussed and aimless, one foot simply waiting for the other to put itself forward. Dropping out was the easy part, sustaining that abstract freedom and endless task. I had barely got it into focus after four years of stoned travels, adventures from a Kafka-esque Kerouac treatise, the reality discerned with magical inhalations which glossed over the evil and immoral. The ability only to react: no thought or plan beyond the next immediate destination, often the next joint would automatically change or enhance the mood of the now. Wide open to whatever fantastically drifted past the iris. The haphazard became the norm, the abnormal became the usual, a freaky awakening from a sheltered suburban cocoon. Avoidance of the critical, of the responsible, ultimately required the lighting of another joy stick, addicting to obviating the true reality, side-stepping the issue at hand with an altered state of mind.

The war hurt, it hurt everyone remotely connected to it. Even now, its tentacles still reach into our collective attitudes, stabbing at our concepts of how we should now handle the emerging new order, the capitalistic road map of consumer frenzy. The other part of that pain leads us to a green awareness, a protest at destruction, of senseless, wanton, ill spent actions. It's the direct link to the middle way to enlightenment, to mindfulness. The being at one with self, life and nature. Everything about the conflict was deprivating, an exposure to all that is profane which man inflicts upon himself and his fellows. War is, however, for those who survive the greatest mind expander anyone can go through. It can be really exciting, even verging on the glamorous, the very edge of the brightest light, death. The spectrum from that light is such an intense glow that it becomes obscenely difficult to focus in on it, to portray it in a way that transcends the vulgar, transposing the horror to a beauty in the same fashion as Goya did. We are but two moments and we never truly experience either; the moment of our birthing and that of our departure from our earthly life. In between, we create a spectrum of stabs at the best we can do in any given situation. War reduces these situations and actions into a virtual blur, freeze-frames what has been so briefly glimpsed: the unavailability to be there at the moment someone close meets his fate, though it may occur merely metres distant. Our fragility, the temporary nature of our sojourn, dawn rapidly, but not at the time, only when the surviving is on line. Witnessing a birth and witnessing death are equally traumatic confrontations with the ultimate, the camera mercifully acting its part a scrim, a filter to the wrenching fear and horror we all have to face.

The lens distils the unthinkable, all that we try to obviate from our daily thoughts, into a form which transcends the impossible so that one can contemplate post factum on the enormity of where one has been. A fast forward film in the past tense lighting up the diary of the moment that would normally be relegated out of the consciousness. Daily, hundreds of people are slaughtered in the name of politics or religion; rarely is their untimely demise recorded; the

documenters who occasionally witness these horrifying events are automatically elevated to a minor heroic status. Maybe we should be stoned for it, put down lest the truth is out and said. Our predecessors and peers were strictly censored, much of what they saw and told censored until way after the cause of the occasion had triumphed. The '60s brought with it a liberating air, a window on to reality was thrown open and promulgated. Photojournalism came of age over night. Communications had speeded up to the point that a dear one's demise half a globe away could grace the front page of your daily or the screen of the television over your breakfast cereal. Reality arrived unwrapped daily, the purity of the images refreshingly shocking and enlightening. Sandwiched by public relations hype that to consume was great now greed.

I grew old fast in Vietnam. The only alternative was to leave, and that seemed silly at the time since the adventure of staying alive was too much fun, the camaraderie of those special friends too intense to turn away from. One peak of experience after another, a continued wave of surf to try to ride to a safe beaching. And always the frames, the contact sheets and proofs, the slides projected to mull over, to ruminate upon the enormity captured, often not in a critical way but more in an *en passant* mode. The obvious made light of to bring it to the bearable, a somewhat sick sense of humour developed to armour-plate the emotions.

'First to know, Last to go', was the motto emblazoning the logo of the TWAPS. The heraldic design consisted of cross pens surmounted by a frontal outline of a Nikon F, then our workhorse camera, letters and gear outlined in yellow on a blue backdrop. 'TWAPS' across the top of the shield was slang for Television, Writers and Photographers' Society, a somewhat louche insiders' hardcore media club functioning out of the press centre on the Song Hong river in downtown Da Nang. The same group of folks who had been jeeped and bussed out to Red Beach for the glorious marine amphibious assault and landing on March 8, '65. Then the only opposition had been a welcoming ARVN band and a bevy of local beauties in their traditional slit-to-the-waist over silk diaphanous pyjama outfits, leis in their hands to garland the flak vested grunts.

The marines were reluctant to trust the press. I guess we made them nervous with our fashionably '60s long hair and indifference to their starched discipline. However, their command had decided they needed publicity and PR they would get. The naissant Da Nang press corps of six to ten folk were offered the opportunity to move into an ex-French bordello/hotel the marines had snapped up happily, with the erstwhile patron as manager; a number of the serving staff elected to keep their boss company. The wire services, AP, UPI, Reuters, AFP, the networks ABC, CBS, NBC, plus *Time* and *Newsweek* and a couple of the major papers all bought into monthly room rentals, ensuring a changing pattern of beds for the ever impoverished freelances. I was to join the latter's ranks late that summer. Initially I had been posted up to I Corps as UPI's photo man – I should say 'boy'. As the war progressed and ink blotted the length and breadth of the country, coverages escalated afoot and we were besieged with an army of safari-suited (tailored by Minh on Tu Do in Saigon) TV crews. The 'Television' of TWAPS was re-designated 'Terrified'. By then we had started to take casualties and the flaming TV people always needed at least three seats on every chopper, the other networks inevitably demanding space and squeezing the regulars off the mission.

I had gotten incountry just over a month earlier than the landings, fresh out of the backwoods from Vientiane, the two-horse shack high capital town of Laos. With the borders closed and the airport and PTT shut, I had biked out of town on my 250 cc Cotton scrambler and pirogued across the Meking to report in front of an astonished guard at the gate of Udorn AFB in N.E. Thailand. As a reward the US news service, UPI, had offered me employ as a staffer in the expanding Saigon bureau at $90 per week plus expenses. Within the week I was upcountry, out in the field covering US-advised ARVN units in the central highlands and recce-ing the terrain around the country's second city and port. My opposition at the AP was formidable: Eddie Adams had come incountry two days after me and was also sent north to cover his old jarhead alma mater. I was beaten before I could even make a frame, though Eddie consistently guided and helped me out and showed me the ropes, so green I could only just about load an F model Nikon! Then there was Larry Burrows, a fellow Brit, possibly the world's greatest photo-journalist – he was to die in a helicopter crash during Lam Son 719 over Laos in '71 with three other photographers. He took me under his fatherly wing and showed me the rudiments of colour compositions.

Adams, who went on to get the Pulitzer prize for his frame of General Loan executing the VC prisoner during the Tet offensive, habitually whipped my arse, not only in getting the picture, but knowing how to get the precious exposed film back to the US and around the world. On our second operation south of Da Nang with the Special Sector Group 1, I had stepped over a tree line onto a panji stick, lightly gashing my foot. Having cleaned up the wound, deflected by the steel shanks in the new-style US jungle boot, I caught up with the HQ group and Eddie. They had a VC with his arms tied behind his back, who was being roughly interrogated. A sergeant produced a bayonet, and stabbed the prisoner in the gut, ripping the blade up. Eddie busied himself making photos as furtively as possible. I froze, and then threw up. Subsequently, the cable in my pigeonhole read, 'Roxy (UPI-ese for AP) running front page NY A.M.s Stop. You same op. Where pix'. That was the last time the picture faced me down, although when confronted by torture and interrogation, an M16 or carbine pointed at one's own gut with a curt 'No photo!' dissuaded further coverage. When the grunt packing the weapon is a ROK, Tiger Division, 'tis better to comply, but by the time he had picked up on my shooting, five frames were in the can.

I learnt to carry one camera with colour, the first E-chromes, Ektachrome then rated at 64 for the normal, 164 for the speedy stuff.

Naively I treated this as though it was black and white and achieved surprising results. Everything was guesstimate. I came home with a large radio battery plastic bag full of trashed equipment field-stripped for parts. In the end, the only survivors were the M Leicas and Nikon Fs: little else could take the punishment. The abrasive grit blown up by the chopper rotors or the culminative effects of a three month monsoon mould and drench. Notwithstanding, the gear was one of the three reasons UPI gave me for the choice of either resigning or getting fired. The other two were: not going out enough, and smoking dope in the photo part of the bureau. I resigned.

By the end of that summer enough marines were ashore to enable Westmoreland to go over from aggressive patrolling to offensive operations. Hoping to snare the 1st and 4th VC battalions on the Batangan Peninsula between their forward base at Cha Lai and Quang Ngai city they threw Operation Starlite. This was the first time the marines were to be deployed by, for them, a massive helicopter lift. The op postponed for three days leaving self and one reporter still around to ride the first assault with 2/3 marines. That way got pinned down in the LZ raining fire zapping us from the heights of Elephant Hill as the amphibious part of the op came in from the east. By the time the platoon and company I had been assigned to had taken the high ground it was at half strength and I would see six pages of my take in *Life* magazine. One incoming 60 mm mortar blew a marine apart right in front of me, wounding two others and lodging three pin hot darts of shrapnel in my backside. I went out with dust-off number five with the body bags to process through the Medivac system, arriving a fêted hero at the press centre at dusk. The perfect scoop.

It was a strange experience twenty years later to return to My Lai, scene of the infamous Americal division's massacre of nearly 400 civilians, to realize that the erstwhile village had been where we had landed that September day and the green hill across the now verdant paddies was that fateful mount.

Within five weeks of that spread, I got caught with the 173rd Airborne, in the 'Iron Triangle', in an ambush where they took nineteen killed in action and thirty-five wounded in action in the five seconds of the sprung trap. It cooked off at almost the same moment that the touring Hello Dolly troupe opened at Nha Trang AFB. The show got the cover and my work went four pages including a vertical double truck inside. My press credentials switched from 'freelance' backed by *Paris Match* and the AP, to *Time/Life*. Regular assignments now were passed out by the respective bureau chiefs of the two magazines' Saigon offices, all at the royal sum of $100 a day plus expenses.

Photographing the Biggles-like adventure, for so it seemed, was a young man's dream. It was addictive, we became junkie moths to the chromed recording of the most perverse, most emotive, most edgelike scene that boyhood novels had ever possibly illuminated.

Overleaf: Orpington, 1979

It had taken months to convince the Cuban authorities that every slice of life from birth through death, and all the in between provisions, should be documented for a tome on their country, an oeuvre befitting their social state, their level of development, and appealing to their proudest, yet profanest, expectations. Many of the aspects needed had to be grabbed on the road during one of the mega swings the length of the island. They included the Instituto Psychiatrico, the Maternity Hospital, militia training, the nickel mines and other sensitive parts of a society that is loath to be investigated. The paranoia of Communism sees suspicion in the normal, and dislikes its layers being peeled back or questioned. This is all in flux as Communism devolves, with erstwhile hardcore states disintegrating and a 'new world order' emerging.

The Instituto Psychiatrico lies out near Jose Marti airport in Havana's suburbs, and looks from the road like a well-heeled state ranch. Its placid exterior belies the bedlam housed inside, though the really secure part where politicos are exiled, Cancer-Ward-style, is off limits. So is the wing where Latin American bigwigs can dispatch their miscreant-addicted offspring to get cleaned up,

secure in the knowledge that there is no deviation from a cure here.

The long barn-cum-workshop buildings house the various therapeutical activities that the different grades of inmate are employed at. The majority appeared old enough to have been here since the revolution in '58, a lot had that staringly awake look induced by a diet of 240 volts at regular intervals. The tasks preoccupying them were, at best, mundane. Putting slotted strips together to hold medical vials apart in boxes. Tearing up rags into small squares to stuff pillows while another group sitting on benches at a table tore identical squares into threads to make surgical dressings and cotton wool. Further along, trusted ones had tools and were building cane furniture, while the prize exhibits, who had a corner to themselves, were allowed to indulge artistic expression. Strange paintings graced the otherwise bare walls while weird sculpts in various stages of completion littered the floor space. For the women there was make-up therapy. Precious sticks of lipstick and nail varnish were given to a pair of old women for them to while away their fantasies. The directress of the institution actually believed that she

'It only hurts when you laugh' or perhaps you only laugh when it hurts.

could release these budding beauticians on to the burgeoning free market beyond the electric fence. The killers and rapists, overseen by therapists with large cudgels, were busy mowing the lawns and weeding. The whole complex was spotless, everything in conformity; nothing untoward or out of place.

It was spooky, for every time I entered a new building the inmates would ga-ga to a standstill from the complexity of the task at hand and glum vapidly at me and the accompanying party. Odd folk, I presumed ringleaders of the go-slow movement, would be whisked off to corrective treatment. After three hours of trudging depressingly round, the missing folks were to be found assembled in the auditorium to give the honoured visitor an impromptu choral performance. The lead baritone singer, a famous ex-bandleader in Battista's days, had been put here, we were informed, 'for his own good'. It was like crossing 'Jazz on a summer's day' with 'The Munsters' show. Out back, the terminal ladies were engaged in dance therapy accompanied by another famous ex-jazz pianist tinkling '50s improvisational blues on an out-of-tune upright piano of the same vintage.

We laugh at others' misfortunes, and doing so relieves us of the fear of being in the same situation ourselves. We laugh a lot as part of the defensive mechanism, we giggle nervously at near escape from danger, at the mirror of ourselves in the sufferer. How else would we survive or maintain a sense of humour? Laughter is not necessarily humorous. With Orientals especially, it is a way of releasing tension. In the direst circumstances, the most gruesome moments, you will see people standing about tittering and giggling, camouflaging their grief and distress. We would probably call this sick; in reality it is relief, it provides a bridge to get on with life, to seek a path to recovery. For in the East, death comes as a release from the worldly, an opening to something better, more replete, an understanding of the finiteness of our short passage in life. Yet it is not mocked; the passage, the path to be followed is absolutely revered, the core of the philosophy. Fear is abated, loathing recedes and the wheel turns. This continuance is part of the symbolism of the Yin and Yang Grin and bear it; lighten up and smile.

Flying in choppers was a dodgy business at best, the whole experience dependent on a flapping blade held on by a series of what the crew called 'Jesus nuts'. More of them fell out of the air than were shot down by Charlie; the mechanical failure rate was double that of all sapper attacks. Still, they were a more than exhilarating experience, the ultimate Biggles trip. The clattering thuck of the blades thumping across the sky will always make me look up; an adrenalin pump goes into gear and all the fears and fantasies zoom into focus. The remembered ride to the front.

Out in the North Sea oilfields, the Pumas and the Messerschmitts, the Chinooks and Lynxes, are the cabs to the oilrigs and platforms. The same cool bravado of the pilots flourishes as in the Nam. Up in Aberdeen everyone on a mission waddles out to their bird encased in survival suits and life vests. Back in the Nam it was all O.D. green, armour-plated vests and flak shirts. The same pucker factor of F22, the same uncertainty, the same rush. So where did the high heels fit in?

Left: Toking the spring away beside the canals in Venice, Ca.

Below: Liberation in '75 had not meant a great deal to the Laotians. (A lot slipped across the Mekong into Thailand.) The warring factions of left, right and centre were all controlled by brethren princes vying for slices of the pie supplied by different nations. The US wanted to control the opium/heroin which the hill tribes cultivated, so they seeded the hills with Special Forces camps. The Vietnamese virtually ran the left wing Pathet Lao, while the neutralists ebbed from side to side, eventually opting for Western largesse.

War only brought strife and damage and, above all, lots of indiscriminate bombing and mine-sowing to a quintessentially Theravada Buddhist state.

The Pathet Lao victory darkened the freedom of the happy-go-lucky land, whose national philosophy is 'Bo Pin Yan' – roughly *Ça ne fait rien*, *Mañana* or *So what*? For once they were obliged to get down to some hard core socially orientated programmes. The wats were initially closed and the monks forced to work. This was not the way of the land of the million elephants and the white parasol (Lang Xane). It was no longer the laid-back place where I had come of age and

emerged as a photographer. Returning for the fifth anniversary celebrations of independence/liberation, I found the mood had changed, the system was breaking out of its dogmatic mould. For the first time in five years, the government allowed the Tat Bat, the annual almsgiving to the monkhood gathered at Tat Luang, to occur. Against the panoply of the most sacred temple in the country, on the December full moon, the whole town of Vientiane came back to life. Suddenly there were no shortages. Coffee, tea, chewing-gum and cigarettes flooded the market. The assembled bonzes got first dip into the once-again-proffered coffers.

Dublin, 1985

Da Nang, 1985

42 degrees on a dusty day down by the Bayamo river
in eastern Cuba. Co-ordinating seven lads is almost as
difficult as herding chickens.

It was Hunter S. Thompson who was quoted as saying, 'the sixties were for the experience, the seventies for surviving and the eighties for paying the mortgage'. I withered in the '70s, surviving with a lot of help from friends. Shell-shocked from the war like many veterans, without aim, without hope, getting by on less than $2,000 a year; too many drugs, too much alcohol and too much violence. In the '70s, my old flatmate from Saigon, Nik Wheeler,

passed me the Sipa West Coast string and with it a glimmer of hope. I covered the whacky events, the weird Californian sub-culture, the figure-eight racing, the military vehicle collectors, the stars' hands in cement on Hollywood Boulevard, the air races in Mojave and the Miss Nude California competition out at a nudist ranch near San Bernardino.

The opener had been the starkers sky-divers.

Cambodia had finally opened up again. There was still fighting going on between the government forces and the Khmer Rouge resistance, but in Kampong Cham, north-west of Phnom Penh, enough normality meant that folks could get back to the restoration of their village temples. The spiritual thread of Buddhism had never been completely quashed by the Khmer Rouge, although they had trashed the Buddha statues and the wats. They had systematically tried to

obliterate all trace of religion or alternative philosophy to their own, and most of the monks went to the killing fields. The people's joy at being able to return to normal is to be found on nearly every road in the secure parts of Cambodia where villagers turn out to block traffic, ransoming the passage of every vehicle for a tatty wad of riels. All drivers carry a bundle for such exigencies, showering the dancers and drummers with the means to rebuild their local wats.

I worked up this theory that the chap is employed by hotels in downtown Bangkok to look for the buttons missing from guests' laundry. Maybe he finds four a day?! Patpong Road and Suriwong in '84.

29

Every country has a national sport, but then, at a more basic level, there are the pastimes of the ordinary folks. The Caribbean and Cuba dominoes rules the streets, a magnet to every underengaged male on every block - a focal point where the woes of the regime are bantered freely. Games are the placebo, the past, the instant arena, winners; losers; the vagueries of life played out.

In Hanoi, every Cyclo driver stashes one under the passenger seat. Most are simply scratched out in the dirt or on the sidewalk. Vietnamese chess is almost identical to the form we know, except that there is a canal or a river running through the middle of the board/battlefield, which only certain pieces can cross; for this they have introduced the elephant. It takes some fathoming and, like the Vietnamese, tends to change each time it is explained.

Autopista, Cuba, 1988

THE BLUES

From one's wardrobe, it is immediately obvious what bias, what predilection exists in favour of a certain colour. Mine ranks blue and more blue.

Jeans served with Oxfords and naval crewnecks, American workshirts in heavy twill, traditional denims, even the socks, both in Oxford and Cambridge, dark and light, chameleon to the sky I fantasise zooming off into, the azure of my mind. Blue for me does not stand for sadness or pain… It is just the air in the sky, the water in and around. Blue is free. Blue sobers, strokes, solaces. It flows, the shifts in its inner spectrum dictating modes, moods of creativity, the workflow. The results refresh, cleanse, the joy of the open firmament, the wide horizon. A colour to soak you up and transport you to the beyond. I feel free in blue, unroled, neutral.

As post-trauma depression, the blues are a photographer's problem. To bore into someone's grief, his despair, his anguish, is always a moral dilemma. The decision to peel away a person's protection, the privacy which we all expect in such profound spasms, becomes the lensman's bête noire. The need to penetrate the emotion, and at the same time to maintain the sanctity of the individual. Few of us can feel comfortable as we seek to strip the dignity off the afflicted, piercing the soulful in virtual perversion, putting the camera's eye to the ultimate test.

I had plodded round and up the heavy cobbled streets (rumoured to have been constructed from the ballast rocks off of New England trade ships) in the blistering sticky July heat of the old Spanish main town of Tinidad on Cuba's south coast. Heaving up the last flight of the stepped street into the piazza in front of the cathedral, dripping sweat, I spotted two men schlepping an enormous neon cross across the top end of the plaza, the broken flex trailing behind them tail-like. The previous day, on an introductory swing through the town, there had been a lovely snap of the cathedral, palm framed against the setting sun, only half the cross illuminated which caused the marginal imperfection. Now here was the shot – a biblical scene – a fused electric calvary. Staggering uphill, framing, focusing, the pulse to grab the image. The photographer's curse was evoked, both cameras in play, ran out of film, and the campangneros with their neon surrealism ran off the frame.

I clumped to the cathedral stairs, plonked down to service the gear, proverbially trousers round the ankles, unguarded, a spliff rolled and fired. As the chrome locked home into the Leica, central casting answered my stoned supplication and sent from stage left the perfect counterpoint to the beautiful sleepy square.

Raised on Capa's images of war, his D-Day frames that had been partially destroyed in their drying, left indelible stains on my mind. The closeness of the terror of death by drowning, incoming fire or both. The cold numbness of the Channel waters seemed to reach from the grainy black and whites. Capa died on my tenth birthday in 1954, victim of a landmine near Nam Dinh in Tonkin, the northern part of Vietnam. This marine landing north of Chu Lai in 1966 was unopposed except by the sea that flipped a couple of the LCMs – killing more than the Vietcong did in the ensuing Operation Colorado.

North of Dong Hoi in the panhandle of North Vietnam below Ky Anh, the estuary of the Song Rao Cai is crossed by a dilapidated ferry, push/pulled by a '60s vintage homebrew tug on a chain attached to a landing craft barge, with hand cranked ramps. During the war, this was one of the prime targets in the bombing campaign against the route leading south to the network of paths and roads that made the Ho Chi Minh trail. The briefing-rooms of the American command would have designated Ba Don a 'choke point', subjecting it to round-the-clock attention either from the aircraft of the 'Linebacker' operation or from the 7th Fleet parked just out of shore-gun range lobbing in high explosive with up to 16" shells. The landscape had been seriously rearranged, though today it looks utterly tranquil; just out of camera are skeletons of destroyed craft and ugly recycled bunkers. Typhoons regularly plague this stretch of the Tonkin Gulf, and afterwards the fishing is plentiful.

The work ethic slots neatly into the blue mode. Few of us are actually able to feed our hearts and minds with gainful employ that we really enjoy. Most of the time we are getting by, surviving, coping with the necessity of maintaining. Not that work is alien, but most of us would prefer to be elsewhere, doing something more selfish rather than having to handle the grind.

A photographer's work is his pleasure, pastime and provider of sustenance – hard to give up for a 'job'.

Little over a decade ago, Phnom Penh had been emptied. When the Khmer Rough entered the city in March of '75, they forced the population to readjust to their concept of Utopia: medieval Marxist gulags with attendant killing fields. A society and a nation came to a standstill. After liberation by the Vietnamese four years later they emerged to start from scratch. Year Zero seems a century ago now, although the city is still without a decent electricity supply or running water and bustling with a million plus new folk, many who have never lived an urban life before, born in brutal camps. On the dyke perimeter road around the city lie belts of different crafts and light industry. In a country where money has only been a reality for the last seven years, and where there is an acute shortage of oil now that the Soviet-bloc aid-missions have gone home, Khmer ingenuity has created the 'remorquee'. They weld up from bicycle tubing a long thin trailer chassis mounted on motorcycle wheels, sling an ornate flat bed body atop it, and hook the rig behind any Honda - preferably a 90 c.c. A maximum count of 20 + chickens, pigs etc., has been noted bouncing along the cratered, pitted, war-ruined, flood-eroded, Khmer-Rouge-neglected highways.

Left: During the 50s, the heavily corrupt American labour unions laundered their monies via the Mafia and directly invested in the then Fascist Battista-led Republica de Cuba. They built casinos, bordellos, resorts and hotels which Castro's revolution inherited. The eyesore on Havana's shoreline is the twenty-five storey 'Riviera' constructed out of the Union of American Workers' slush funds in the mid-50s boom. It peels and cracks through lack of upkeep, the tourist guests queue in the self-service canteen for a school-dinner-standard refuelling, and sleep in damp beds. Meanwhile, the enormous workforce occasionally get someone off their siesta-attitude to put in a modicum of maintenance. Draining the pool was probably part of Fidel's next five-year programme.

After the Cuban revolution, the enormous foreign-owned sugar-cane plantations were nationalized overnight. The island's staple crop became the people's, with the people obliged to turn out in brigades to reap their economy. The Cubans invented a Rube Goldberg-like machine to harvest the cane. It is still a major part of the economy, but has been surpassed by nickel as the major export earner. The CAI (Centrale Azucar Industrie) Antonio Mella, in the province of Holgain, Fidel's home state, was one of the first repossessed by the state. Although highly mechanized, it still relies on First-World-War-vintage, ex-Panama-Canal-construction steam locomotives to drag the cut cane to the mills for refining. This happens in the heat of January.

Cuba is a rolling motor museum, the American colonial trace resplendently represented in a plethora of '50s Detroit iron. Cubans will willingly pay five times the price of a new Lada to own a '58 Buick 88 in a country where gasoline is strictly rationed and expensive. Per capita income is less than a thousand dollars and the Russian vehicles at knock-down prices cost five years wages. This '59 Cadillac shines in the driveway of middle managers' '50s-built housing in the main sugar terminal of Cienfuegos on the south coast.

The state also nationalized property in Vietnam. The French in '55 lost an entire colony with its carefully orchestrated plantations. Their 'Indochinoise'– styled buildings reflected both the home nation and the affluent colony. The former Metropole Hotel in the middle of downtown Hanoi became the Thong Nhat and proceeded to decay for three and a half decades. The plumbing was, at best, French, the wiring a nightmare – dangerous spaghetti, often connected to the aforementioned pipings. The *ascenseur* never worked since its installation in the '30s, and the same rats had been breeding ever since, producing progeny the size of well-fed domestic felines. The lobby was their playground, the appalling restaurant's kitchen their power source. It had a faded elegance, a *charme manquante*, a whiff of colonial decadence, incredible woodwork in the palatial rooms that had housed the elite of the erstwhile empire. Besides, it was the only place in town, the other hotels being models of E-bloc mediocrity and inefficiency. Now a consortium of French companies under Pullman's banner has bought the crumbling edifice and is restoring it to a new glory. Under Doi Moi, Vietnam's *perestroika*, private enterprise is encouraged and thriving, foreign investment encouraged. A room for the night in the Metropole will cost the equivalent of six months pay packets for the average Vietnamese.

An almost audible sound of relief escaped from America when Watergate burst upon its collective psyche. The whole rotten, maggot-ridden core of the corruption in politics and justice was laid bare. The open wounds of the Vietnam war could be examined. Dan Ellsberg and Tony Russo had illegally copied and distributed the Pentagon papers, the definitive white paper on the war, opening the can of worms even further. They were put on trial at the Federal Courtroom in Los Angeles in 1973, and the case dismissed after Ellsberg's psychiatrist was burgled by one of Nixon's dirty tricksters. At the height of the trial, the two regularly attended spontaneous rallies and demonstrations at the courtroom plaza.

In the People's Socialist Republic of Laos, Pathet Lao, it was always hard to figure out who were the winners or losers. Five years after liberation in 1980, the country still ranked in the bottom ten of the poorest nations globally. Vietnamese advisers still sat at every ministry desk and the true spirit of the country was only just starting to emerge once again. For the glorious fifth birthday, clothes and uniforms were issued to the populace, while the market was swamped with rare consumer goods such as the locally produced cigarettes and beer, formerly exported to fraternal Socialist states. An enormous fair and expo were organized, with obligatory march pasts and parades glorifying the revolution. The entire cabinet and staff of the military were on hand for the five day bash, which must have accounted for a quarter of the GNP.

It was a sad day, a day of exorcism, catharsis, revelation. For the day before, up in the high mesa country of northwest Colorado, I had finally got to remeet the sergeant who had lost his legs on top of the 350 lb anti-tank mine that fateful 19th April back in '69. My parents had exchanged Christmas cards with the Hokes, but my trails had never led to the mountain state. Visiting Bill on his 40-acre ranch which he ran single-handed from horseback, ATV and pick-up truck was a link in my own recovery from PTSD (post traumatic stress disorder). My blues were being swept away by confrontation with the past. Then clear light before the raging downpour and storm over Gunner while driving south to Santa Fe crystallized the emotional release.

The orthodox Theravada school of Buddhism practised in Thailand has been somewhat degraded by the demands of the twentieth century, leaving a state of philosophy veneered with McDonald's and Coke, and Thai yuppies regularly going on retreat replete with mobile phones and portable TVs. The purity of Buddhism has been heavily corrupted, with many monks setting themselves up in profitable non-profit cult-enterprises within their own wat walls. Some are even proselytizing the harmony of the military-run state and the church, virtually propagating militarism against the precepts of the dharma. South-east of Bangkok, outside the now horrific resort which was once the small fishing village of Pattaya, is a huge walled temple complex presided over by one senior abbot monk (thero) Kittibukku. After the closure of the nearby USAF B52 base at Sattahip, he somehow got the contract to round up all the left-over vehicles and construction equipment. The wat compound is a sea of old ambulances, school buses, 'hiabs', cement-mixers and scrap. Young bonzes puddle concrete, learn radio communications and repair, fix trucks, preparing for posting to wats situated close to the then contested borders of Laos and Cambodia. Affluent, influential, devout families send their sons here for the traditional period which every male must pass in the sangha.

Maybe it is the small-boy syndrome, the lure of far away battles and adventures in remote, exotic locales, but ever since I was able to grasp a historical perspective, Dien Bien Phu, the site of the battle that sealed France's Indo-Chinese fate, had been near the top of the list of places I wanted to go to. The visit, finally, in 1985 was, as expected, anticlimactic. The two-day trip up to the valley high up in cordillera fastness had been spectacular, the road a torture for the GAZ jeep, with landslides, washed out bridges and only just edible food. This part of Vietnam is one of the poorest, with only occasional flat lands or terraces to afford cultivation. After the battle in '54, the government settled a number of the men of the divisions who had fought there to populate the wilderness, simultaneously subduing the local ethnic mountain-dwellers. Three generations on, the strife had evaporated and their offspring, with a virtual lack of birth control, constitute a greater danger to the country's welfare.

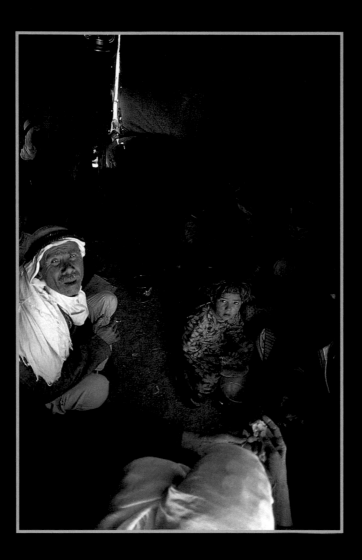

It must have been 120 degrees F. inside the old army tent stuck out in the desert at Mafraq on the Jordanian/Iraqi border. The first Bedouin and Palestinian refugees trucked there were in no mood to complain, thankful to have escaped alive after eviction from their West Bank camps and homes.

It was the only train running in the entire
county. A good proportion of the passengers
were the Saigon Press Corps, flown in for the
day on a propaganda junket to show how
well the countryside was under control. A
work train was to head south from Phu Bai
station and base to where construction crews
were renovating the track on the line to
Danang. We thought that they maybe hoped
to start a commuter service for the peasants
to get the twenty kilometres to market in
Hue. Another ploy to prove the war was
being won. The return trip from the railhead,
the twenty-year-old French loco pushing the
string of boxcars and wagons, was incident-
free, but nervous ARVN troops perched in
doors and on roofs, lounging GIs guarded
bridges and culverts. Just as we were back in
Phu Bai's perimeter those of us in the lead
anti-mine gondola car were presented with
the image of four startled white eyes peering
out of black faces, inside the cab of an
American gas-bowser about to cross the
railroad track. You could almost hear the
stoned rap, 'Hey, man! Hey? Lookee! A train!
A real, live train! Hey! Wow, man! No, really
man! Dig it'. It was a slomo accident, one of
those where you watch your own fate
cartwheel. They stalled the gas-truck four
square upon the railroad-crossing and the
train had only one course at a steady 15kph.
The truck flipped over, the lead three cars
derailed and started to plunge down an
embankment. The guard in our gondola
continued to blow his whistle and wave his
white warning flag throughout. It could have
been worse: the GI's had broken legs, I broke
a finger trying to leap the three metres over
the car's side as it lurched off the rails.

Mini-Tet, the sequel to the New Year's offensive of 1968,
launched by the Vietcong, was heralded by a blast heard a
kilometre away on the café terraces in downtown Saigon.
A taxi stuffed with 500lb of plastic explosive had been
blown up right outside the armed forces network television
station. Unfortunately, most of the blast took out the
neighbouring Vietnamese/American student association
building, leaving the TV station just heavily shrapnel-
pocked and windowless. 'Gunsmoke' and 'Combat' – the
in-country favourite shows – would still go out uninterrupt-
ed. Meanwhile, the rescue services started to pull the
obvious bodies from the wreckage under the watchful
lenses and eyes of the international media. The initial
casualties were quickly extracted and the press dispersed.
Intuition told me that they were going to find another body
at the bottom of the wreckage. It took another hour to get
the earthquake-pancaked building-rubble peeled back to
reveal the crushed form of a teenage girl.

A million people crammed into a square kilometre in the piazza of Fatima in front of the basilica for the fiftieth anniversary of the vision by a twelve-year-old girl of the Virgin Mary. The seething mass was not consoled by the prospect of Pope John's arrival and the faithful were dropping like flies in the crush, leaning forward in dense packs towards the grandstand that overlooked the sloping cobbled square. For three of the four days of the pilgrimage it rained - it poured - and the masses began to emit a fetid smell: piety mingled with that of candle wax, damp clothing, stale bread, garlic, wine and urine. To cross the horde was impossible; one had to circumnavigate; plunging into it was a half day assignment.

The last chopper ride in-country. The bird seemed to be
flitting *ad lib* around the III Corps border area with
Cambodia. Firstly, I had to get the free market on film,
then on to a fire base that had been hit to pick up some
intelligence documents, then back to Bien Hoa with the
papers. En route we had to stop at a forward operations
base of the 25th Division and drop off two peasant
women who had been blithely cycling back home from
the market when our jumpy door gunner had unleashed a
burst from his M60. Naturally, they took evasive action,
another burst and they awaited our descent to scarf them
up for the ride to an unpleasant interrogation at the base.
Half an hour later the same chopper was diverted to a
dust off mission; two GIs caught by a bouncing-betty
booby trap needed medevac. The top-sergeant and myself
leapt out to effect the pick-up, I snapping nervously.
Then the mine blew. The rest is another, confused, story.
I still wonder what happened to the two innocent lady
farmers.

Overlying the putrid smell of the body in the casket, there was a reek of hot wax and incense. A keening filled the Catholic cemetery, the women mourners in traditional white grouped at the coffin. Their priest, who had led them south in '54, had been run down by a threequarter ton MP truck. It was a good time for the Catholic politicians to demonstrate their disquiet at the US decision to call a bombing halt to North Vietnam and their discontent with the Ky/Thieu clique then in the driving seat.

Now, I am not astonished or surprised, only saddened by the number of unfortunate people who still cannot be provided with prosthetics in Vietnam. Just when you think it is starting to look normal, O.K. again, another wrecked body heaves into vision bringing back a feeling of despair, of wanting to help, but also of inability to grapple with the immensity of recovery. Trackside in Ninh Binh station, the pickings for a beggar from a first-class train on the up-line could yield a reasonable reward.

Down an alley, almost opposite one of the habitually used opium dens of the early '60s, I finally found a people's democratic liberated fumerie. The government had decreed that only those over fifty could be addicts. The old habitués had clustered in a stilted shack of bamboo and scrap, surviving on a thin weed and noodle soup and endless pots of green tea. My man's son worked in the hospital, ensuring a steady supply of the golden black brown liquid, keeping his 106-pipes-a-day habit together. The paying customer who left cartons of Marlboro must have made this Lao OAP's day! Vientiane floated by outside, a murmur in the afternoon heat, the honey smoke wafted solicitously into the original oriental dream.

The mountain-dwellers have experienced a strange dichotomy. Once they were oppressed, suppressed, prejudiced against and classed as savage; now they are integrated to the extent of being trusted in the local militia. You might find him packing an M16 – part of $4·1 billion worth of material left behind in 75 – a weapon he might well have used as an ancillary for the special forces patrolling the perilous stretch of Route 7 linking Ban Me Thuot to the Cambodian border, an area still alive with small resistance cells.

The middle of Cuba, once a forested rolling countryside, so densely wooded that early Spanish explorers said it was possible to traverse the island without seeing the sun, is now arid cattle country: the meat larder of Fidel's proclaimed socialist Utopia.

The provincial capital is the old Spanish city of Camaguey, started in the late 15th century, which boasts the largest slaughterhouse in Latin America, and is home to the Ballet Classico Folklorico, the national troupe. That day in '89 we had done the abattoir before breakfast and the art before lunch. Beast and beauty, food for the body and soul.

We got out of this Huey in a hot LZ south of
Da Nang with the HQ unit and US advisers and
immediately had to take cover in a bambooed hedge
line, the 60mm shells plopping down, spraying
shrapnel negligently around our heads. The ranger
two metres along the ditch grinned nervously and
as one groped to proffer cigarettes of relief, I lost
and stoked up a foul ARVN-GI-issue imitation
Gauloise and he got to use the slid back Zippo.
I hasten to add this was all done at leaf mould level.

Inescapable eyes binding you to the guilt of their suffering. Pain, fear and loathing, mutilation, the end, death.

Facing the unfaceable, trying to face being drawn back. Peeking over the edge of the precipice. Diving in the emotional deep end.

Is it that, once seen, you want to pass on the lesson of the horror? Or is it simply the fear that we will all forget our fragility? The avoidance of looking profanity in the eyes and being able, almost, to mock it? How will it be for the self, I wonder? For the Buddha said that only two things are constant – change and death. Beyond the evil we do unto each other, we are now sometimes more intrigued by the evil we do to our environment, the beauty we once inhabited.

We bore morbidly into the gore, somehow seeking in the blood red slashes an answer to our sins. The putrid becomes a carrion feast for our fascination; interrogating these phenomena photographically becomes a perversion. A war photographer becomes the most perverse. The label sticks for ever. If you accuse someone of it, he denies it hotly.

Staring at the horrors now, the repulsions forced back like rising bile. The obscenity becoming mythical, twisted adventures. The surreal in spades.

Pathos ripping at your throat threatening your vision. Unwanted, obsessive. Hatred and horror. Finally humility.

Haunting, going back out again, junkie moth in a searing flame, trying to fix Goya on everyone's collective mind.

Hopeful that the image can change the way we perceive, the way hopefully we will then perform.

The cutting edge softened for consumption.

The A10 North American Thunderbolt, also known as a warthog, is designed to withstand punishment on the erstwhile Eastern European combat front, suppressing Communist armoured spearhead columns and bridgeheads. The pilot sits in a titanium armoured tub atop a GAU 9 multi-barrelled 30mm Gatling cannon, firing depleted uranium at 6000 rounds per minute (reloaded by an ALS – auto reloading system – in a matter of minutes) beside a selection of wing-pod mounted rockets, CBUs (cluster bomb units) and homing missiles, both air-to-air and ground-to-ground. The tub ejects in case of a fatal hit to the high, rear-mounted, quiet jets. You can barely hear it coming. The Iraqis and several friendlies were to find this out in the Gulf. It can even survive in an NBC (nuclear, biological or chemical) warfare situation. It can clean up: period. The pilot wears a suit enabling this, called Darth Vader.

Once a year, Time Inc sponsors the Time/Life businessman's tour of a planetry region or continent. 1968 saw the mega-corporations' top honchos wheeled around South East Asia on a Rent-a-707, including a look-see at what their dollar was doing for the American industry, and, incidentally, the Vietnamese. On the third day of the tour they were packaged up to Cam Ranh bay kitted out in spanking new fatigues and boots, belts – the works. Here they got live demonstrations of their products and the men who grooved them. The seals were about the hardest of our hard corps, cross-trained SAS special forces, Scuba airborne ranger – the whole bit. They looked really good and lit up a mountain with tracers for the men from Mars.

Left: Somehow during the
Six Day War, I got posted
by Time/Life to the, then,
backwater Beirut, rather
than the gung-ho state of
Israel. After eight days of
lapping up George Hotel
four-star life with anti-
Western riots as a work
frame, we drove down to
Amman to cover the stream
of Bedouin refugees being
evicted from the newly
occupied West Bank
territories. The wretched
folk were leaving with only
a bundle or cardboard valise
to be rehoused at Mafraq on
the Iraqi border, in a stony
desert in ex-army tents.
The roads out of the Jordan
valley were littered with the
pathos of their escape.

New Year '69, having an *oeuf sur plat*, *café au lait*, at Brodard opposite the
Tu Do flat, when a civilian engineer working Bien Hoa airbase, 25
kilometres north of Saigon, burst in, announcing that two photographers
had already got zapped in an action at the end of the runway. The North
Vietnamese had tried to spring the inmates of a nearby POW camp, had
gotten beaten back and made a last ditch stand in a Catholic church. The
whole unit had been wiped out when dawn came and the helicopter
gunships could make merry. By late morning the blackening corpses of the
enemy had been limed down for common burial. In theory, lime prevents
the spread of disease and repels flies.

Strolling back from a light, French lunch at
the Romancho, down Nguyen Hue boulevard, ambulances and emergency vehicles
blocked the way. A crowd gathered, fascinat-
ed. Two double agents holed up in a fifth
floor flat had decided to top each other with
grenades. No winners in the contest, no further questions.

The Combinado Carnico de Camaguey is boosted by the state authority
concerned with meat production as the largest abattoir in Latin America.
It daily processes 550 cattle and a slightly larger number of pigs in the
most humane and hygienic way I have witnessed - chilling, yes; upsetting,
marginally. A necessity in the rolling cattle and cane country that
dominates the centre of the People's Democratic Socialistic isle of Cuba.
They offered us breakfast in the works canteen, ham, corned beef, stale
bread and strong coffee. I was with my ex-wife and it was our second
wedding anniversary.

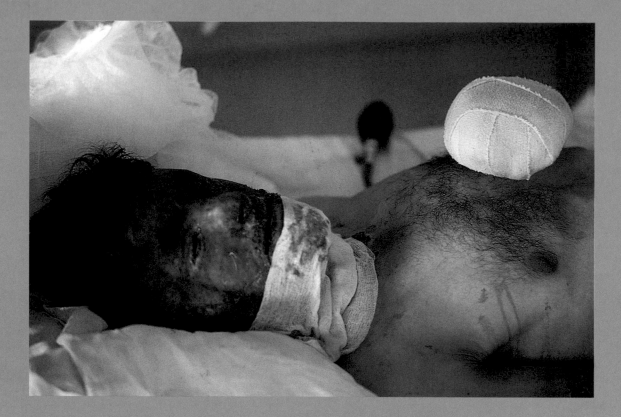

Rushing to re-enforce the fighting on the East Bank and Jerusalem in the Six Day War, the Arab legionnaires, King Hussein of Jordan's elite division, were caught in their soft-skinned transports by the Israeli airforce. With no air cover of their own, they were sitting ducks to the napalm and CBU strikes. The mutilated casualties were repatriated to Amman courtesy of the Red Cross/Crescent via Cyprus, to be put on display for a few of the world's press.

Also on every hack's itinerary when visiting Ho Chi Minh Ville, formerly Saigon, is the orphanage for children - victims of the defoliant Agent Orange. Eleven million gallons were sprayed across South Vietnam during the American epoch, to deny the enemy cover from the air. Triple canopied forests, dense jungle, scrub, were reduced to a not-so-slow death by denuding all their green bits. In calibrated areas, including paddies in disputed zones, most of the country got a dose to deny the Vietcong food supplies. The horrific stuff seeped into the water table and thence into the local inhabitants. The effects are passed on genetically through the male, and the incidence of strange cancers has been dramatically increased, with many offspring suffering mutations and deformities never before witnessed.

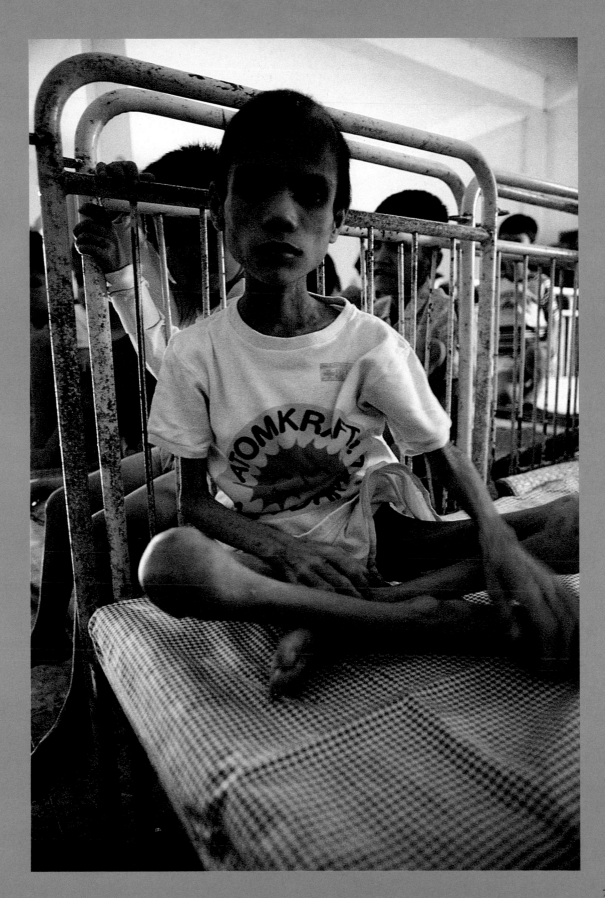

The poor woman is a nurse and had lost her first three children to miscarriages. This time she was determined, as were the staff at the largest maternity hospital in Havana, that the birth would be a successful natural one. There was a collective energy willing the 23-year-old on in the pre-natal ward, and then beautifully in the delivery room. The daughter weighed in bawling at seven and a half pounds. The threshold of pain pushed to the ultimate orgasmic pleasure.

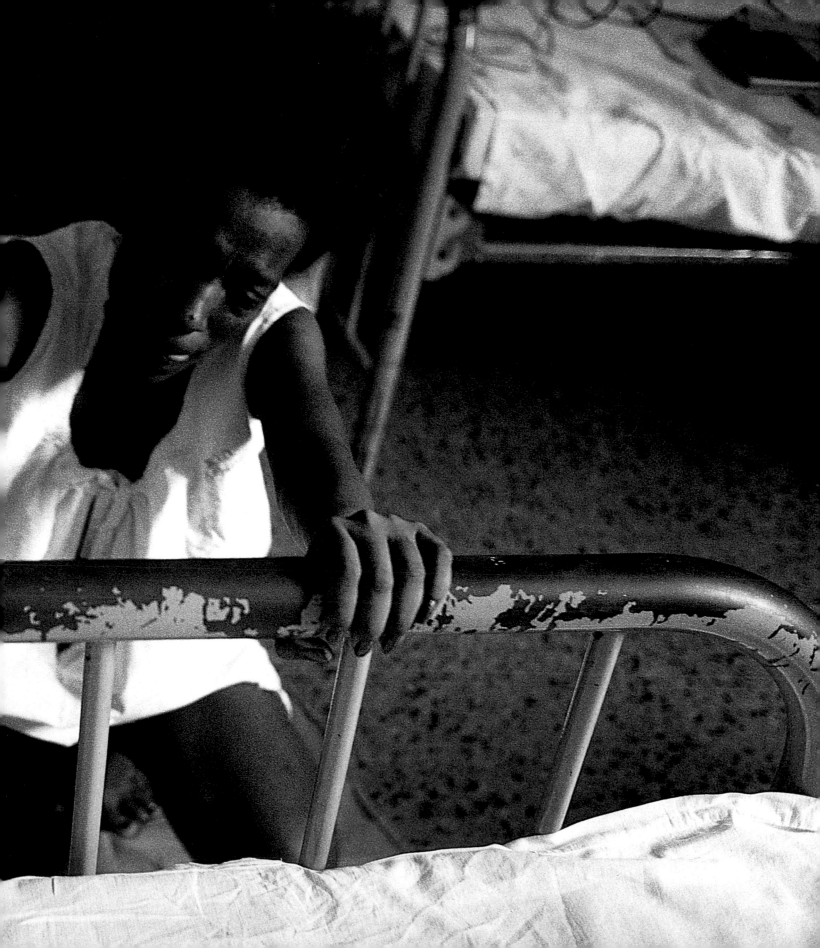

In neighbouring Cambodia, where Prince Sihanouk has just returned to head the new SNC (Supreme National Council) in the officially decommunized nation, the Americans have accredited a special envoy with ambassadorial rank. In theory, the four various, once-warring, factions have equality in the UN-engineered government. However, when Khieu Samphan, the Khmer Rouge leader, returned to take his seat, a government-sponsored crowd rioted, sacked his house, nearly lynched him, and forced the loathed Khmer Rouge delegation back to Bangkok only hours after its arrival. No one was arrested for breach of the peace, restraint of the crowd was minimal, and the UN had obliged the new corrupt regime to accept their statutes. The Khmer Rouge were now back in Phnom Penh in a more secure house, fighting resumed in the provinces and the first UN peacekeepers arrived to attempt to keep their mandate. Soon, it was hoped, the millions of mines littering the land would be de-activated, and almost half a million refugees return to their homes.

P.S. The elections were a success as a shaky peace prevails across the state of Cambodia, Sihanouk crowned as king, and once again the Khmer Rouge have been obliged to leave town, their party now disenfranchized.

Illegal immigrants ('I & Is') trying to get into Hong Kong barely touched their dreamed-of land, before they were diligently scooped up by the Royal Hong Kong Regiment and the Gurkhas. The troops go I & I fishing at dawn in the new territories, nabbing the half-drowned swimmers in the Lo Wo salt marshes from small Gazelle helicopters. It is an impossible flood to stop; many of those captured are repeaters of the tenth order.

Those perpetuating the pain in Toul Sleng must have had the bizarrest sense of pleasure possibly imaginable. In the old French Lycée, the classrooms had been divided up with breezeblocks to make 2 x 3 metre cells where the prisoners were held in between their sessions of confession with their Khmer Rouge interrogators. The system consumed its own leaders; the top persons requiring special attention were deliberately singled out for savage abuse. The pervading air of the Nazi concentration camps lurks in the foetid air of the erstwhile school.

Places of death, hanging trees, killing fields, have
a universal feeling; a vibration; an ambience that
can never be dispelled. Battlefields fall into
the same category. I suspect that from time
immemorial, painters and photographers have
imagined the same wasted feel imparted by a
section of the planet fought over and desecrated.
We are fixed by Fenton's Crimea, Brady's
Gettysburg, by the madness of Flanders' trenches,
by Capa's D-Day beaches. The bleakness of
Khe Sanh at the end of the '68 campaign gave
off the same, used beyond hope atmosphere that
thousands of other sites had previously endured.
The military command in Saigon tried to make
us believe it had lured the North Vietnamese
Army into the remote Annamitic Cordillera
fastness to blitz them back to the Stone Age.
The reality was the opposite. The Marines
hunkered under heavy Russian-made incoming
artillery parked on the inaccessible, inclement
weathered mountains, dependent on a logistic
tail engaging thousands. The North Vietnamese
Army, meanwhile, popped their Tet offensive,
the rear areas of the free world being only thinly
guarded. Khe Sanh was another hell in a small
place destined for history because of the tenacity
of the Marines and an eager media corps.

Covering the Six Day Middle East conflict from the Arab side was not feasible, deadlines in New York impossible to meet, the film arriving circuitously late, access to the fighting virtually prohibited. One was left with post-action scenarios to cover. The Israelis obliged by expelling all the Bedouin out of the East Bank territories, in their first wave of contra-Palestinian-Arab harassments. The pitiful refugees, clutching hand luggage, were trucked out to the inhospitable desert astride the Iraqi-Jordanian border, to a spot marked as Mafraq on the maps. Later the camp was to become a cauldron of Palestinian revolution, crushed by Hussein's legionnaires. I thought of Capa's frame taken in Israel in '48 of an almost identical refugee, that time, ironically, a Jewish immigrant.

I didn't notice the stump on the tree, I was too busy trying to understand the ex-guerilla's apparent grin (or was it a grimace?), too preoccupied to really listen to his story being recounted by my interpreter in the background. This was a whole camp of mutilated ex-fighters, the losers in the battle of El Salvador, left wing Farabundo Marti liberationists pitted against the American-backed military junta. Their main actions had been bombings, their technique dubious at best. Three years previously, at 15, this lad had been injured by a premature explosion on his way to an assignment. Eventually the Red Cross brokered a flight of all the disabled to a neighbouring hospitable patron - Cuba. Here they festered, frustrated, on a small farm 45 kilometres from Havana, last heroes of a forgotten revolution. A footless American marine Viet-vet arrived monthly to cast their limbs for prosthetics; illegally, for Cuba, too, is embargoed.

Three years later I was to meet Dave Evans - the same veteran - building limbs for Cambodian limbless former soldiers at the Keng Klaeng clinic across the river from Phnom Penh. Indo-China's amputees are the highest percentage in any population worldwide. Some of the one-time liberation front soldiers and North Vietnamese get prosthetics, some get wheelchairs. Most of the old regime troopers end up with neither; relegated ex-puppets and pariahs. Pyle, in Graham Greene's *The Quiet American,* must have driven over the same road as this former Vietcong fighter on his journey to Tay Ninh.

Hanoi, 1990,

RETURNING

Coming home is now the prime joy of the assignment, the fulfilment of my trip.

Going out in the field was, and still is, the most difficult thing to push myself to, testing, testing, testing. The first trepidatious step out of a chopper, that M25 rat race fast-lane flyway to Heathrow or Gatwick, the gnawing feeling in the pit of the gut, a hollow, queasy bile-laden sensation. The signs of fear, once beaten back, re-emerging. Again the frailty of one's body as a temporary blob of flesh and blood, energy and bone, made painfully transparent. You kid yourself by careful preparation you can obviate disaster; you plan, you meticulously pack, carefully stash the delicate, the important. You go over all possible eventualities and portentously meditate upon the incense sticks you light for the Buddha before departure. The refugee must feel the same alienating grip of panic going into exile.

Coming back to the verdancy of Britain is munificent, the first plane window downcast sweep revealing ancient field patterns in hues of green, ranges of trees and the road, railways and rivers appearing model-like, dinky toy in size. The quaintness is in the eccentric non-patterned nature of its layout. Nobody fleeing conflict ever has the benefit of even a random select of order to look forward to. Perpetually their haunted visages haunt our vision, they keep returning to our pages and screens. Inevitably, as a photographer bent with journalism, I have to document them. Pathos guarantees the images that editors head for.

Somehow, though their fate is the same, the refugees encountered in the Far East seem to have an easier lot than their brethren forced out in the bleakness of the arid zones. Coming away from the Middle East after six weeks of the Six Day War, my eyes felt seared, traumatized by

the surreal nature of the juxtapositions of humans against the harshness of the desert, dumped there after their forced exodus from Israel as it expanded its frontiers. At least the poor souls on the Thai/Cambodian border had too much water half the year; the folk who braved the seas off Vietnam saw too much of it. Maybe it is possible to get blasé about them, overdosing on the empathy, digging deeper into the compassion collective, only selecting that which will push the pathetic into the unforgettable on film.

It is good, healthy and somewhat selfish to foray into madness and be able - at virtually one's discretion - to bug out of it and return to the pastures of sanity. I return now to the weather-swept crest of the North Downs in my native county of Kent (was it not Thomas Wolfe who expounded the theory of that battle 'or you can't go home again' and the reasons for doing so?). Many days, walking out the front or back door of the cottage can be likened to stepping into one of Turner's paintings. For all the Medway lies a mere ten miles to the north. The skies brush the crest forecasting fronts and depressive troughs, and when autumn and evening close in and there is no light, I can retire to blazing fire and comforting book. Escape to the privacy of closing the door to the outside, the retreat to the cell, recentering before another sortie, another adventure at the coal-face. Going out to photograph these skies is a tonic in itself; the experience of using a camera as a brush, the film as paint. Plodding along the ridge beside the poplar windbreak, the weather becomes unimportant. I meld to the sky, a flight path opens upwards and I soar. The rush of fresh air, the being at one with nature, with the self, with life - this is coming home, this is the inner calm that home is supposed to be.

Arriving back out in the East, in South East Asia, is the other homecoming. The familiarity grabs me instantly, the heat sucks me

Preceding pages: Cayo Guillermo, 1989

Kampot, 1991

up, the learning curve has begun once again. Here, where formative years were passed, is the easy key to self-discovery; the universal world of the Orient and its overlying Buddhist philosophy. The alien was encountered nearly three decades ago; now it is like sliding into body-warm water, it re-envelopes immediately, stimulating all the dormant mannerisms and perceptions. Though we are hardly graceful by the local standards, and any photographer stands out like a Christmas tree, though we are uncouth, tall and white, I always feel chameleon; I take on a different skin, emit a different aura, become purer to self and fellow man. The images fall into frame, the Zen of being at one with my camera-self. Then I find I am home again, the gnawing fear of the transfer a passing pain. The real joy of this return is the friends you must continually be re-acquainted with, with whom the past becomes richer, the nostalgia deeper. Fantasies are shared. Images just created are tried out upon that hardcore of friends, of buddies, the welcome shrink-cum-critics of the most personal.

Returning to the site of a photographic campaign is like returning to the scene of the crime, like re-meeting an old lover. It recaptures certain magic, a main line to the emotions of the past, now to be improved on. That philosophic thread, once woven back in Laos in '62-'64, the first glimpses inside the Siddhartha path, are now part of the pattern in every shoot. Going back to that root, where it had all perchance started, has proved the most cathartic experience of all, re-opening the third eye to the beauty of life, to tranquillity. It was as though I had never really been away; I felt total familiarity to the nuances of one of the more eclectic spots a traveller could ever hope to be. Back in those formative years, the early '60s, when my peers were busy beavering away at careers or in colleges, I was experiencing life under the dictum of Bo Pin Yan. Finishing the pre-hippy overland trip in the then unfashionable destination of Vientiane, I was launched into the perceptions that only the Orient can teach, learning to balance, blend in and accept the fates. It is all a sort of swimming lesson in the benign deep end of the pool, where the beatific can infiltrate the conscience at a leisure unknown (even then) in the frantic so-called civilized West. Only later, when the various familial factions started once again to take up arms against each other, was I to witness photographically the darker side of ourselves. Those first scoop snaps introduced me to the world of photo-journalism inside a wire agency. The stupor of Laos was rapidly exchanged for the insanity of the escalating conflict to the east in Vietnam. Somehow, though I had remained in Indo-China for the best part of five years, I had not returned to my fount. Vietnam, and a brush with death as close as it is possible to experience in the war, the subsequent invaliding out of the zone in mid '69, and the seemingly endless recovery from those traumas, removed the feasibility of ever getting back to it.

Eventually, in 1980, the *Observer* Magazine dispatched me off to South East Asia. The bug which had been planted almost two decades before was re-awakened. At first it all went wrong, like a cyclist who has not gotten on two wheels in ages. I wobbled and fell off and disappointed myself. The shock of re-entry to the amenable balanced world after too long on the West Coast of the States and of the drab UK made it hard to attune the mind as it had done before. Returning to the East would be my re-awakening, my revival from the turgid self pity I had ensnared myself in since the war. Returning to Laos was to be the first creative rather than retrospective step I would make in my re-birthing, the new phase of self-discovery. Going back to Vietnam for the earlier two weeks assigned sojourn had been pure catharsis. The softness, the pastel tone of Laos was still there, fulfilling expectations as it also marked its fifth year of liberation as a socialist state. The wars that had chewed Indo-China to bits in the '60s and '70s were half a decade gone, and with it the first flushes of retribution and revenge. Laos was coming out in the first celebration of Tat Bat for a decade, an alms-giving ceremony to the monks of the land by the assembled populace of the Vientiane plain. The walls of Communism were cracking with the spiritual re-awakening of this erstwhile 'liberated' nation. Neighbouring Vietnam and Cambodia were still enchained with dogma; their return to the normal was still years down the track. Revisiting Laos provided a new key, the ability to express the gap between East and West, the dichotomy of the two, Comrade Lenin meets the Buddha. The philosophy observed and vaguely adhered to over the years since I had first encountered it gained an ascendancy; a certain dharma focused in my mind. The photo-quest could turn into a pilgrimage, a homage to the guidance that I was now awakening to, the world where the wise took up the saffron robe and appeared to live in a harmonious existence with both themselves and the world about them. That world centred on the sangha of Buddhism. It had returned from being a besieged minority to open acceptance in the DDR of Laos and still encased the people in neighbouring Burma. Even in Cambodia, the evils of the Khmer Rouge under Pol Pot had been unable to stamp out its spirituality. I was probably returning to a faith, a set of values, that had seeped aboard in my post-adolescent stay and that could now open lotus-like with the new light I could now interpret. Orange, brown and saffron in many hues will continue to ripple my mind whenever I travel the pilgrimage on endless quest for the ultimate enlightenment of nirvana.

They also originated the break to a new destination, entering the world of serendipity, Sri Lanka. A short list of sacred sites, ceremonies, shrines and temples for an illustrated book on the world of Buddhism, plus the incentive of a guide-book, led to a nearly two-month invigorating sojourn trying to complete an impossible task. The island's dimension has probably suited us Brits, from tea-clad mountains to the arid north, lush jungle and plantations to paradisiacal beaches. The beaten-up Peugeot 404 had done almost 8,000 kilometres with nearly 150 rolls of chrome consumed. Finally, only four full moon ceremonies (Poya) had not been covered, and the eleven months of four visits had passed oblivious to time or mileage. For in Lanka it had been possible to put together another home away from home up in the botanical gardens overlooking the bowl of Kandy's lake. Steeped in the lushness of primal jungle, the colonial villa of English friends became more than a base camp. Awakening here was a meditation in green. Even the trees appeared to be in conversation clamouring at the myriad insect and bird calls. A pure nature call. I used to go out with the complete scheme already in my head, bent on filling in the missing pieces of the jigsaw. There were to

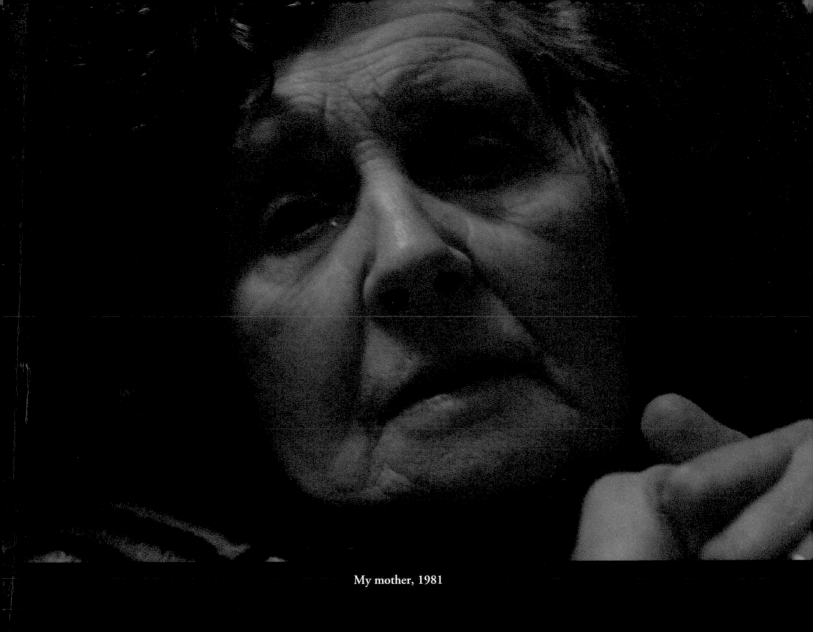

My mother, 1981

be six essays, following a new Zen line I was learning. After each sortie I returned to the light-table to edit what I had taken. The photography was hard work, but the real test was the selection, picking out the superlatives from the merely super, finding the quintessence of one's own tastes. The peace to do this ebbed from the energies of each successive visit to the different monasteries and shrines attempting to capture their best in the diverse seasons, trying to catch the perfect illumination. Coming back to the UK this time was an anticlimactic downer: my heart had stayed in the emerald isle with its purer form of Buddhist practice.

Parallel to Lanka had been the Burmese magnet, another Theravada land, another culture following the orthodox school of Buddhism, that of the lower vehicle, as opposed to the Hinayana school of the Himalayas. I had traversed Burma in '63, a lucky visa facilitating a three-week passage. I had been entranced, and now I was going back for a yearly dosage, again focusing on its pure form of philosophic adherence. Oscillating between nostalgia and rush, forever confronting old emotions, strengthened rather than weakened the imagery. The new, after all, was not unfamiliar, nor the familiar surprising. Memories zoomed my consciousness with unnerving frequency.

The decade of pain, searing bouts of fear, loathing, confusion and mindlessness, the dead years of the '70s, had been passed mainly in the United States. The accumulated hang-ups were now removable; a warmth seeped into the soul. Returning to the countryside and its enveloping green seemed to exorcise the war once and for all. On 30 April 1975 Saigon was liberated; the North Vietnamese immediately rechristened it Ho Chi Minh Ville; ten years on, the anniversary prompted a massive celebration. It also signalled the opening of the country to the West by the hard-core Communist regime and to facilitate this emergence they allowed the free world's media to flock in to document their decade of progress. It seemed the ideal time to celebrate my own recovery and take advantage of the facility being proffered to the assembling six hundred newsfolk. In the end it required five months, three visits and 18,000 kilometres of rough road to finish my book *Ten Years After* and then another half year to whittle down the 650 rolls of exposed film. Coming home was anticlimactic, the wave of shooting had been condensed and yet the ride long. Old ghosts had been exorcised, chased out of nightmare into creative imagery. Time and again, familiar places or names had loomed into vision, but their capacity to unsettle me, their fear-inducing, negative energy was constructively turned round to create memorable images.

It was good to have put Vietnam aside, to retract the damaged undercarriage, but I was still aware of the junkie pull, the hypnotic spell the Orient had sowed in my soul. I changed face and headed west to the New World again, the Latin American one. North America, specifically the east, and then for almost a decade the West Coast had been a sort of home. An innate obstinate false belief somehow had made the US of A responsible for my dilemma. Because I had been on an assignment for Time Inc. when last zapped, the 25th Division had made me an honorary member for the incident, so logically

compounding the myth, I was an honorary citizen. I had even married an American citizen, believing matrimony would add a dimension of security, of commitment, which then did not exist. However, I never managed to cash in on any of that, only achieving a vortex of violence and self destruction and eventual deportation. Those problems reflected mine and the nation's attempt to recover from the trauma of the Vietnam conflict. The United States was now a place to visit for minute spasms: preferably *en passant*, in transit. Too many raw nerve endings had been exposed for any sojourn, too much respect lost for a society bent on consuming itself to extinction.

Re-entering the British way of life, albeit laced with inefficiency and eccentricities was, after turning mid-Atlantic, nothing but refreshing. Back in touch with parents and a separate sense of balance.

South of the border I had just touched on the Latin in Mexico but had never ventured further into the main. Cuba slotted exactly into the concept of a challenge. The enduring revolutionary image of Che Guevara still hung in any '60s-raised mind. Fidel's effrontery and adherence to a socialistic path was now an isolated, insular example. The Communist bloc was changing; in the Soviet Union *perestroika* had caught on; the Viets had inaugurated Doi Moi, a restructuring and opening up. A magazine assignment for *Elle* dissolved in two weeks into a Glasnost o Che. The island and its society *de*pressed, but more *im*pressed, and the hook was set. There was a bright new interrogative beat to the frames, a new set of colours to manipulate. The Caribbean was an integrated melange of creeds and cultures. Treated as royalty, access ceded where none had shot before, I found it the perfect *volte face*, the ideal alternative proving-ground for all that I believed I now could comprehend and document. Going back to Cuba those four times was more refreshing than cathartic. The experience left intact those feelings, mainly spiritual, that the Orient had implanted. I had already been twice to Panama, once on a de luxe basis for American Express, once ending at the blockade of a Noriega citadel in the Darien Gap. But those visits did not enhance the lure that Latin America had held when I first left home at seventeen to find a path. Cuba did reinforce – what the Buddhistic countries had sewn in my mind – the need for a more socialistic solution to all our dilemmas. As with Sri Lanka, a Brit is attracted by the insular, the island syndrome, the ever-changing sea-sculpted skies scudding across any vista. The light captured over the cayos off the north coast of Cuba could be tropical Turners, an echo of the walk that daily started on Windmill Hill overlooking the Weald. Those ever-dissolving skies become my sanatorium – a weather eye on my sanity. The breaks in the cloud-fronts were like breathing-spaces, helping me in the dogged labour of editing and writing, overcoming my mental blocks.

Finally I got to ride the train of my dreams, the reunification express between Saigon and Hanoi. Even though it had been the first essay of *Ten Years After* it had been shot from afar, never aboard. It took thirteen days, off and on, to make the story, lingering in Da Nang and Hue, retouching magic after a four year absence. The story was writing/shooting itself, the very being in-country the tonic of creation, the mind open to vibrations that had been shelved too long. South of Da Nang, beyond the now infamous ex-Marine R & R

Praying for peace,
Dao Island, 1968

Bomb victim, Vientiane market, 1980

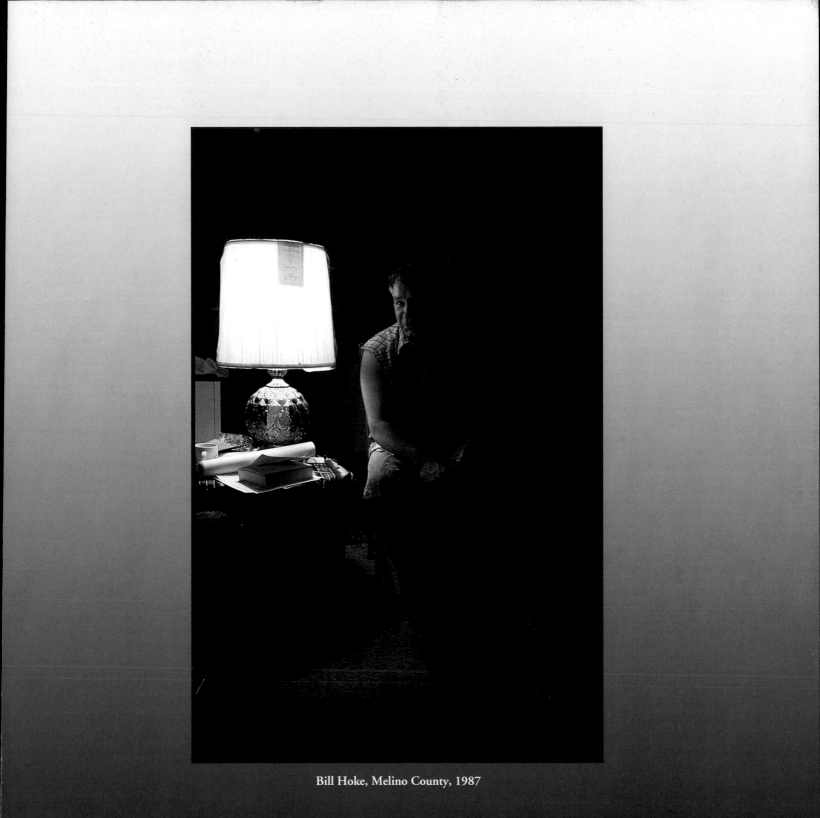

Bill Hoke, Melino County, 1987

Looking at Flynn's picture, Beimet, Kampong Cham, 1990

China Beach, rises a cluster of jagged rocks, mini-peaks covered in scrub and jungle. In the marble fastness of this heap dominating the flat paddies of the Song Hong valley is a sacred grotto, with an image of the Buddha in Samadhi carved from the back wall of the cave.

During the war with the enormous III MAF (Marine Amphibious Force) sprawling northwards away towards the city, the dolomitic crags harboured a Vietcong unit who sniped randomly into the vast complex. Divinely protected by the Buddha against outright assault, the mountain complex was definitely off limits. My brother in photographic arms, Sean Flynn, and I would go to meditate in the cave beside the trickle of Vietnamese civilian pilgrims. It was one of the few isolated places of peace in the war-torn land. It still is, the grotto pierced by shafts of light stabbing through the roof holes, the incense in the porcelain vase on the altar in front of the effigy swirling towards the ceiling, a soft drip of water somewhere, a cathedral presence. It is eerie, it is slightly spooky, but definitely a place of the spirits.

Those spirits – nats, pis, whatever language has them – are to be paid homage unto. To believe they do not exist is to be out of harmony with the environment – not only discourteous but actually dangerous to one's welfare, inevitably leading to an imbalance of one's own dharma, the path. It is customary to light incense (here in the Nam called Huong) to please them.

Visiting the cave in '89, I did so, retiring to the damp descending entrance stone stairs to meditate upon the eternal space. There, somehow suspended, virtually indescribable, they glimmered, shone, hovered. I wondered whether they might be Sean's spirit, but none of them exactly fitted. Maybe we draw ourselves psychosomatically into feelings, into seeing the invisible. Some believe in ghosts and the supernatural, some prefer not to. I vacillate in conviction. What I was seeing was an energy, not at peace, not directioned, having no abode, no place to rest.

I should explain that Sean and another close photographer friend, Dana Stone, had disappeared, captured on 6 April 1970, riding Hondas east from Chi Pou in Cambodia towards the Vietnamese border, looking for the Vietcong/Khmer Rouge. They, and another seventeen other media personnel, were never heard of again, though the bodies of a few were accounted for but never recovered. The later horror of the Pol Pot years distracted attention from their fates. A few lucky co-correspondents survived short spells of captivity, proving that in risking the adventure to get the story it was still faintly feasible to return home from the impossible. Since then in dreams, Sean's spirit had appeared clearly in colour, talking in his laid-back way, quite distinctly, the ordeal now forgotten, the stories continuations of conversations from 47 Bui Thi Xuan, Paris or the apartment on Tu Do in Saigon we had co-habited for three and a half years. Half-stated stoned vignettes buzzed back and forth in the field had, in the dreams, been finally completed. Our pact had been that should either of us go KIA, MIA or be seriously shot up, then we would notify each other's next of kin. He had, when I had gotten my near fatal mine-blast to the brain. And I did the same for his mother after getting the news third hand while living down and out in Hollywood, reaching

her before officialdom or Time/Life, for whom the boy was shooting at the time.

That October in '89, in the calm of the grotto, the presence was undeniable. There was no communication, only an unsettled feeling, a pained expression. It really spooked me. An hour later, I almost drowned, caught in a heavy offshore current off the resited China Beach. Vietnam Du Lich (tourism) have built a ferro-concrete complex adjoining the southern end of the sweeping bay of Da Nang to accommodate the new wave of foreign tourists as well as the Soviet crews and technicians using the US engineered airforce base. The post-monsoon tides rip offshore at the apogee of the curve, and just after the hour of my near-demise, some Mig pilots were swept away. The helpless, near total panic feeling, the death premonition, had all flashed by once again, to be subdued in a last breath and stroke while Khua, my interpreter, had waved and screamed, powerless on the waterline a mere thirty metres away, soundlessly. Death in Da Nang Part III, spooky shit.

Back in Kent, a mound of mail, another joy of returning. Delicious feeling of old contacts renewed: the brown windowed envelopes last consigned to filedom, business, and then the surprise ones. For a couple of years, a French student doing a dissertation on the media in the Vietnam war, had been in correspondence. Among his case studies was Sean Flynn's life, work and times. This young man's research had unearthed, through the Freedom of Information Act, declassified CIA and DIA reports pertaining to our lad's captivity and subsequent death. The documents all zeroed in to a section of Cambodia in the province of Kampong Cham, near the Mekong river, 140 kilometres north east of the capital, Phnom Penh. This first concrete information, combined with the spooky visitation in the cave, prompted the organization of a trip to the area. Besides, it would be the first time back to Cambodia since National Day celebrations in '68; as well as adding more pieces of the jigsaw, the touch of Theravada, my personal pilgrimage, could be graced.

So I was back in Indo-China a mere two months after the co-incidental happenings with another train to ride the length of Vietnam and a limited budget from another book contract signing, on the bus to Phnom Penh. The magnetic lured me upstream to within twenty kilometres of the spot pinpointed by the intelligence papers, at the two wat village of Khroch Chmar.

That night, gliding back downstream to Kampong Cham town, surrounded by a purple and orange sunset, a dream was born in the clarity of those backlit colours. I know that I should come back and build a stupa on the site of their burial. I just knew it was to be; all the vibrations were in tune.

Maybe we are destined to have only one pure-lit thought in our existence. This was the moment to seize. Here was my cause; a search was coming to a conclusion. I returned to Hanoi and the then foreign minister, Nguyen Co Thach, asked me to found a media faculty at the University of Hue. It was then that the Indo-China Media Memorial Foundation was born, a body that would honour the dead and missing of all nations and perpetuate the knowledge that we had gained in helping to bring that conflict to a close. It would be a college

Washington D.C., 1986

Ben Hai, 1991

advocating peace, with fellowships bringing budding media personnel out of Indo-China to host-countries that had lost men there, who would return a reciprocal number to understand the East.

An old friend suggested resiting the memorial itself in a more accessible place, where we could all get to; for all, Kampong Cham is still not exactly secure. The idea to build it on the 17th parallel was agreed to by all consulted, the perfect fulcrum on the map on Indo-China, as overlaid in a Yin/Yang fashion.

Late 1990 saw the fruition of the first part of the project. With John Sheppard of Granada TV at the helm, directing the documentary, a crew of us set out to the grave site in Kampong Cham. Aided by unseen hands of fate and by incredible luck, we managed to trace Sean and Dana's first days of capture in Vietnamese hands. For the next six months we have no information. Then they resurface, handed over to the Khmer Rouge, with whom they survive for almost a year, before being executed by blows to the back of the neck with a hoe. Numerous peasants patchwork the story together, culminating with a grave robber who produces three teeth and a filling. These are later analyzed as having come from a tall man and a short one, the tall one having expensive dental surgery. An approximate date of death is established, as well as the fact that they both met violent fates. The various corroborations held together. We had solved the mystery of two of the nineteen MIA journalists in Kampuchea.

Upon our descent to Phnom Penh, the chief Buddhist abbot of the now re-emerging state of Cambodia, presented me with a small Bo tree grafted from the oldest sacred tree, a five-hundred-year-old specimen growing on the Phnom (hill) in the city of the Penh. Four days later beside the Ben Hai of the old demarcation line twixt north and south Vietnams, in the company of two stuffed car loads of local luminaries, we planted the thirty-centimetre descendant of that under which the Buddha had achieved enlightenment 2543 years before.

In spite of meandering vociferous goats and three floodings in saline water during the year's typhoons, the tree has grown to nearly two metres high and, late last year, we placed a cuong (shrine) inside the guard fence next to it, and inside that a white marble Buddha copied from the one in the cave. The reason for returning to central Annam has now been forged for ever.

The same spiritual force emitted from the memorial site emanates from the black marble wall in Washington D.C., the Vietnam Memorial with the names of the 58,000 Americans who perished in the war etched into its matt black surface, trapping the observer in his own emotional reflection. Its simple starkness slashes the ground in a gentle V-shape, forcing the visitor to confront the darkness in his own soul. Its design, by the Chinese-American woman architect Maya Lin, leaves spaces in the chronological listings to update as casualties move from MIA to KIA status and as others are reclassified. Finding a name on the wall, a face, is each time a confrontational trauma, rediscovering times carefully buried away, though the need to rake through the ashes of nostalgia is forever tempting.

Wilpattu, Sri Lanka, 1983

100

Chelsea Embankment,
London 1982

Pages 104-105:
Windmill Hill, 1987
Pages 106-107:
Windmill Hill, 1991

Kampong Cham, 1990

Vientiane, Laos, 1980

Do Son, 1990

Colombo, 1983

What am I doing here
Chasing ghosts that no longer see
What is really now or then
Only a shadow of things
Exorcised, forgotten, forgiven
A stream of kharma conscious
A void of sneaky little questions
Kicking in a stoned mind
Seeking balanced lines in east and west
Fucking Nam! Fucking Nam!
Why does it not depart
For me at least in Vietnam
A future for us all to contemplate
Elaborate the inner better.